Introduction

I sometimes ask myself why I started writing these articles. In a space already crowded with many good resources, what new voice did I have to add? What readers were I hoping to reach? What level of notoriety was I aiming for, if any? It's been helpful for me to remind myself that I wrote most of these articles over a two-year period simply because I had to.

I thought I was in good shape after leaving a strategic consulting firm where I spent years learning and implementing the tools of business building. I joined a venture capital-funded startup that needed to determine the next major path for growth. And there were fifty employees that needed to quickly contribute to that decision-making process and align around the outcome. The questions for us at the time were:

- How do you determine the next major future paths for growth?
- How do you know what we can uniquely build and what customers will buy?
- How can you inject data and analytics into products to make them relevant to C-Suite users?
- How do you align employees around the new direction?

We were successful enough that three years later, a larger company acquired us and I found myself in a lead corporate strategy role for a large organization with multiple products, buyers, and office locations. My team and I were charged with building a strategy from the framework that they had already aligned on. Questions appeared again:

- What, exactly, is a strategy? What are the fail-proof steps we can take to build one (while many eyes are on us, the clock is ticking, and everyone wants to know what the process is and when we'll be done)?
- Is "international expansion" a strategy? (It's not; that's an idea which doesn't yet identify who our specific international buyers will be, what their critical needs are, and how we can uniquely serve those needs.)
- How much customer research needs to be done before we can call something a strategy?
- How do you realign a large organization around insights that challenge the status quo?

Then a few months later, strategy reappeared again in a new form: some colleagues and I founded a new company. A new round of questions appeared:

- How do you take a blank sheet of paper and build a new product and company?
- Why us? Why should we believe we are uniquely positioned to build anything?
- How new and innovative should the idea be?
- How do you go into a room, demo a product to a broad set of different stakeholders that serves a need none of them have ever considered before, and, one hour later, have everyone believing that, from this point going forward, they can't live without what we built?

In addition to all these questions, as a student of strategy, I wanted to know how what I was reading (e.g. Michael Porter's books on strategy) informed these questions. What was the one universal theory to strategy, innovation, and business building that tied all of these concepts together and gave me a discrete set of how-to steps?

In short, when I said that I wrote these articles because I had to, what I meant was I needed to capture and structure all of these threads, with all the lessons I'd learned along the way, and document them so my brain could be cleared out to make room for new challenges.

. . .

As a builder of analytics-based products and companies, I often think of my role as the ragged mediator between investors, engineers, and customers.

On one side, analysts and engineers build things while investors help pay their salaries. You can call this labor and capital. On the other side, you have customers who need to be reached out to and given a message that compels them to buy and use your product.

Strategy is the organizing framework that allows you to connect these stakeholders and make the whole process run.

. . .

My lifelong passion has been building products and companies that are powered by data and analytics. Executing the data and analytics work has been the easy part; knowing how to turn that work into a product that solves a need has proven more difficult. I was fortunate to have had the opportunity to learn the fundamentals of strategy while a consultant at McKinsey & Company. Since then, I've been trying to put everything I've learned to work by growing, founding, and sitting on the board of analytics/tech companies.

I wrote the first few of these articles after my colleagues and I sold our last company. It was a good time to go through my notes, ideas, and personal lessons on strategy and remind myself of the fundamentals and how to apply them. And then I started a new company, learning many more lessons along the way—new ideas for fundraising, building a sales engine, and getting to daily product usage. Those steps were all stronger and easier because they were grounded in strategy.

My focus is on three areas: product strategy, analytics, and agility. Analytics is particularly interesting to me in the startup world as companies can leverage it as a source of competitive advantage relative to less data-savvy incumbents. In addition, a strategy that is not continuously informed by data and analytics nowadays is likely to be a weak one. On the topic of launching analytics-based companies and products specifically, I believe I have something new to add.

. . .

This book includes the four articles of "4 Steps to Develop a Strategy" plus three introductory articles on strategy that have been published on The Strategist (strategist.blog).

What is Strategy?

After many years as a data-oriented software engineer, I joined the consulting firm McKinsey & Company. It was there that I got my real education in business building, executive communications, and strategy.

McKinsey for me was a masters' class in strategy from some of the world's most experienced and thoughtful practitioners of it. In my later years at the firm, I helped form an analytics-based startup there and then left to pursue a series of my own startups.

While what I learned from those experiences has helped me tremendously in all of my later ventures, I recognized that what strategy means had to be reinterpreted to apply to an analytics-based startup. The core elements of a strategy as it applies to a Fortune 500 executive team are fundamentally the same as those for a startup. But for a smaller company, strategy needs to provide a path from a blank sheet of paper to a profit-generating product—as opposed to getting the most out of existing products.

In other words, what I've come to realize is that there are two types of strategy.

There are two types of strategy

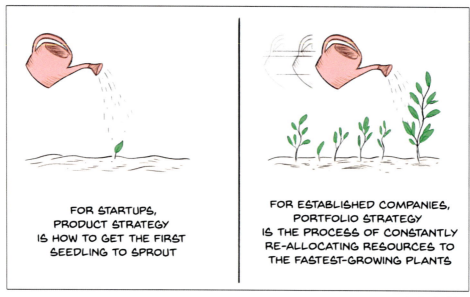

FOR STARTUPS,
PRODUCT STRATEGY
IS HOW TO GET THE FIRST
SEEDLING TO SPROUT

FOR ESTABLISHED COMPANIES,
PORTFOLIO STRATEGY
IS THE PROCESS OF CONSTANTLY
RE-ALLOCATING RESOURCES TO
THE FASTEST-GROWING PLANTS

strategist.blog

"Product strategy" is the process of creating and sustaining a new value-creating product

A "product strategy" captures how and where the product will grow, whether for a startup or a hundred-year old brand.

Product strategy is a simple coherent answer to the classic questions: Who is the buyer? What is their need? What is stopping the buyer from solving that need? What unique assets and skills will we bring to solve it? And how will we delight the end user?

In a startup, this is done by the founding team, the company's strategy lead, and/or the lead engineers/product designers.

"Portfolio strategy" is the high-level process of managing multiple products

For an established company with one or more existing products, "corporate portfolio strategy" builds on top of product strategy.

Innovation and product strategy form one lever you can pull to grow and cultivate new seedlings.

The five other levers within portfolio strategy include the constant re-allocation of resources to growth areas, active M&A/divestitures, doubling down on capital investment, continuous productivity improvements, and brand differentiation.

Active acquisitions can be a great mechanism for an established company to stay innovative. It's a way to keep the CEO in front of new ideas and to avoid a corporate mentality that all the answers they need exist within their own four walls.

In established companies, this type of strategy is typically done by a Chief Strategy Officer or leader of business development; these are roles which, in my experience, are often more focused on M&A than on product strategy and innovation.

Portfolio strategy can be considered a "strategy of strategies". It should answer: What do we create uniquely well? What are we known for by our customers? What are the different ways we deliver what we do uniquely well (e.g. our products)? Which ones are the most promising and thus deserve the most resources? How do our products interoperate, cross-sell, and contribute new value to each other?

For example, Disney's unique skill is creating animated characters (e.g. Cinderella, the Little Mermaid, or Buzz Lightyear) and stories that can be easily ported over to other products such as theme parks, books, comics, and cruise ships. Apple's unique skill is creating well-designed, mutually-integrated, and easy-to-use products with a similar consistent interface across computers, music devices, and phones. My prior company's unique skill was creating tests and e-learning content for clinicians, which we ported into pre-hire assessments, onboarding programs, and personalized professional education.

There are two levels that strategy can operate in, but, in either case, the goal of strategy is to define how you are going to create unique value for customers.

Product strategy, in particular, declares how we will solve a specific need in a unique way

A strategy identifies a buyer, their need/value pool, our chosen mechanism for addressing that need and why it will be effective, the unique skills/assets/capabilities we have, and how all those things will come together to uniquely serve the buyers' needs while delighting our users.

Good strategies also …

- Focus us on the few big decisions (many made before serving a first customer) where our collective effort will be multiplied to create the most unique customer value.
- Force us to zero-in on a particular buyer, their needs, and the tradeoffs inherent in building a specific solution for them, and therefore makes it clear that there are many customers and initiatives we will *not* pursue.
- Highlight the challenges we face and demand real problem-solving power to help overcome them.
- Show how we will build fast-product-feedback-loops ("learning loops") into the product to continually learn and increase the tempo of value creation for our customers.

- Are simple to understand. They are cohesive, coherent, focused, attainable, and clear. They have the outline of real steps we need to take. Anyone in the company can understand them, remember them, explain them in their own words, and apply them to their decisions on a day-to-day basis.

By choosing how to uniquely serve your chosen customers, you are forcing tradeoffs. Aldi (related to Trader Joe's) chooses low prices as its primary mechanism for creating value for its customers. To do that, it has a much lower selection of products (2,000 items compared to 15,000 that many grocery stores have), among other no-frills decisions. What if customers want more choices? That's fine—Aldi is happy to have them go somewhere else. It is instead focused on serving the customers whose needs match their value proposition.

Some decisions and tradeoffs have to be committed to and locked in early on. But ideas that can be tested without irreversible investments should be. Your strategy should still declare the good faith intent to those areas but only with a small investment. Keep your options open for a commitment once you've learned more and reduced the risk.

Strategy is also the path by which a company survives evolution

 [The aim of strategy is] to improve our ability to shape and adapt to unfolding circumstances, so that we … can survive on our own terms.

— Col. John Boyd, the pre-eminent military strategist of the 20th century

The nice addition that Boyd makes with the line "survive on our own terms" is connecting strategy to evolution. Boyd was a student of the sciences and believed that organizations, like organisms, move through cycles, interacting with their environments by learning, adapting, and aiming to survive.

In short, if you win, it is in part because of your speed, focus, flexibility, and agility. Arguably these are more about culture and tactics than strategy—but your strategy should enable and set the groundwork for your ability to shape, adapt, and evolve.

4 Steps to Develop a Strategy

Step #1: What's a High $ Pain Point that Keeps Someone Awake at Night?

This is Step 1 of "4 Steps to Develop a Strategy", focused on identifying a buyer and a value pool/pain point.

A STRATEGY DESCRIBES WHERE AND HOW WE'LL SERVE OUR CUSTOMERS:

1. **BUYER + $ VALUE POOL.** WHAT'S THE HIGH $ PAIN POINT OR UNMET NEED?
2. **HOW TO UNLOCK THE VALUE POOL.** WHAT'S KEEPING THE VALUE POOL FROM BEING UNLOCKED? HOW UNIQUE IS OUR CHOSEN METHOD?
3. **WHY US?** WHY CAN'T 2 COLLEGE KIDS DO IT? WHAT TRENDS WILL WE RIDE?
4. **USER + HOW WE WILL DELIGHT THEM.** WHAT ARE THE 2 TO 5 UNIQUE AND MUTUALLY-REINFORCING ASPECTS OF OUR SOLUTION?

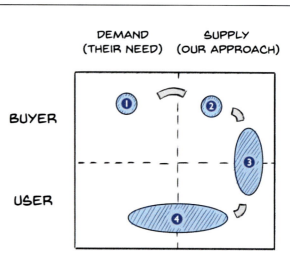

DEMAND (THEIR NEED)   SUPPLY (OUR APPROACH)

BUYER

USER

(1a) Identify a buyer

Anchor on a customer (or start with a few and aim to narrow them down to one). Whom would you be selling to? What organizations do they work for?

For example, your customer can be the marketing departments of large corporations (as it is for Facebook and Google), COOs of hospitals (as it is for manufacturers of operating room beds), or busy professionals (as it is for Blue Apron). The best customers are ones you and your founding team know well. My personal experience is that later, when you're building a product, raising money, and selling a product, there's so much less risk if you can say "I've been serving this customer for over ten years and I personally know their opportunities and challenges."

Too often I talk to other entrepreneurs and, in describing their target market, they say, "I'm building a toolkit that can be used by other people to build businesses in many different industries". That's just shorthand for saying, "I don't know who my buyer is, nor how I can create unique value for them, and therefore I have no strategy."

(1b) Identify a high $ value pool

What's the pain point (or untapped opportunity) for the buyer? How big is the $?
The next step is to identify the areas of highest cost savings or revenue growth potential for that customer; often these are well-known.

A value pool is the $ amount representing how much you and your buyers expect your product to alleviate a major cost driver or open a new revenue opportunity for a customer. Ideally, it is one of the top five items on a C-level leader's mind. Finding a large $ value pool is important. Investors have a saying that the success rate of companies is the same whether they go after a big market or a small one, so invest in those that go after big ones. I use the term "value pools" and not "markets" because product strategy focuses on building new solutions; the term "market" implies that many competing solutions already exist, which may not be the case.

You can go after value pools that potential buyers don't know about, but that requires educating and convincing them of a problem before you can convince them you can solve it. One example of this in recent years was that nurses and physicians communicated about patients on their personal phones which were not secure. With an aggressive inside sales outreach, one secure messaging company made CIOs aware of this and so they then became concerned about the potential risk and urgency of not putting a fix in place. This path can work, with investment. I've been in sales meetings with potential C-level customers where we had to convince them of the size of the problem or opportunity and it's too easy for them to say "it's not a big $ item here". It's just easier for people to not to do anything unless there's internal pressure to do so.

One way to identify the top items is to interview leaders of the organizations. Ask them what keeps them up at night. What are the financial KPIs they measure and are rewarded on? Also, read the publications and surveys that represent them and their roles.

Why bother to talk to them? You need to hear buyers tell you, in their own words, their goals and challenges. Looking outside-in, you may see a lot of perceived inefficiencies in someone's life but because you think a value pool should be there doesn't mean that the buyer acknowledges it.

Unlocking a value pool for a buyer typically means increasing their profits. That means either you have a product that will help them increase their revenue or decrease their costs. A major hospital system once shared that they prioritize revenue-increasing products over cost-reducing ones, but both are top priorities.

The value pool may be unsolved. You need not know how to address it at this stage. A value pool you've documented is one already on a path to being solved.

How big could our impact be against the value pool?

For an established company, early financial projections can be made and various buyer/value pool/chosen method combinations can be contrasted and filtered against these goals, such as specific revenue or ROIC thresholds. For a startup, the rules of the game are simpler: is the revenue opportunity large enough to justify going after? Can we grow reasonably and profitably?

Find the people whom your buyer is most concerned about. Look for value pools by helping them reduce costs or create future growth opportunities for those people

Isadore Sharp, founder of the Four Seasons Hotels and Resorts, wrote in his book (*Four Seasons*) about an early development deal he won with Bell Telephone. "You're investing all this money in future employees—people you hope will make a successful career in your company. Instead of a dormitory why not upgrade their accommodations? Give them a pleasant experience of the company and a good night's sleep, so they wake up fresh in the morning, eager to learn. We can design it and run it in a way I'm sure will pay off." My own experiences have shown that finding the people (e.g. new hires, middle managers, and other employees or customers) whom buyers think about the most is a great way for an entrepreneur to find value pools.

How easy is the value pool to measure? Who is "on the hook" for it?

The best value pools are ones which buyers are already measuring and reviewing every month. Examples for businesses may include metrics such as too many hours spent doing X, too high of a product return rate, too high of a customer churn rate, or too few sales leads.

Who on the CEO's team is accountable for the value pool? If it's an area that's measured today but no one is personally held accountable for it, you may find the lack of a buyer who will clamor for your solution. One such example could be employee turnover. Is the VP of HR on the hook? Or are the individual managers? Or is no one? It may vary depending on how the CEO allocates accountability.

Second best are the value pools which are abstract, noisier, infrequently reported, or harder to measure. For these value pools, it can be hard to know if a solution deployed against them is having an impact at ninety days, or even a year in. Examples of these more abstract categories might include: doctors not being prepared enough for rare medical events, employee happiness and morale being too low, and customers not being aware of a buyer's product. These may keep a C-level leader up at night... but how are they measured and how can we prove that our product will generate an improvement on them over time?

How will we be able to prove our impact if the metric that measures doesn't hover at a consistent, predictable value before our implementation? If this is the case, there may be proxy measures that everyone agrees are correlated with this outcome for which we can show an improvement on.

One example of a proxy measure is customer satisfaction scores for customer retention rates. Imagine you are trying to sell a grocery store owner a product to reduce their customer turnover. While customer retention rates may jump up and down depending on many factors, if you have a product that improves customer satisfaction scores (something the buyer can easily measure), it's a small leap for them to believe the product is also improving their retention rate. The size of the value pool is the financial improvement the buyer expects from the product.

As another example, the value pool of avoiding a once-every-five-years oil disaster may not be measurable every year by the drilling company. But they may use improvements in their team members' knowledge of safety protocols, which is more measurable, as a proxy. You may also have to invent your own proxy measure and sell it as the industry standard, a topic we'll return to in a later article.

Not all CxOs have equal buying power

As a general statement, it's been my experience in US hospitals that if the CEO really cares about a topic, funds are allocated, RFPs go out to find ways to solve it, and products get bought. CEOs really care about publicly reported metrics and anything that is tied to reimbursement.

CIOs and CFOs typically have a lot of purchasing power as well. CNOs have a lot of purchasing control and influence on labor spend but typically much less so on IT purchases. CHROs own a few core IT systems and vary greatly in their interest in being innovative outside of those systems.

In other words, define a buyer as a specific role in the organization and understand that role's typical ability and interest in buying products like yours.

Will the value pool grow and persist?

Is the value pool likely to remain unsolved five years from now? Is there a time limit like the fixes for Y2K had? Is there an obvious solution that everyone will have implemented soon?

The question of how the value pool will change (i.e. Grow? Shrink? Persist?) is often overlooked. It's harder to get an insight into, but interviews with forward-thinking buyers should illuminate the most likely trends. For example, TiVo was a company in the early 2000s. It allowed cable and satellite TV viewers to pause, delay, or record TV shows that were live-streamed for later on-demand viewing. The customer need was that people wanted to watch content when they wanted to, not when TV stations broadcast it. But the massive trend was in content becoming internet-based and on-demand. That trend removed this value pool and there was no obvious replacement that TiVo could pivot into.

I was talking to someone at a kid's birthday party recently and shared the criteria above. I realized it was a lot to remember so I said I should get it printed on a bumper sticker to help. I decided against it, but I tested out what it might look like.

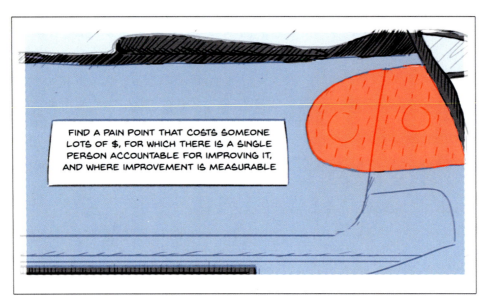

FIND A PAIN POINT THAT COSTS SOMEONE LOTS OF $, FOR WHICH THERE IS A SINGLE PERSON ACCOUNTABLE FOR IMPROVING IT, AND WHERE IMPROVEMENT IS MEASURABLE

BUMPER STICKER ON A STRATEGIST'S CAR

strategist.blog

Expert interviews are gold for finding value pools

I rely heavily on interviews. The questions you might ask include:

- What are the top 3-7 metrics that your organization measures to track your business's performance?
- Which metrics are revenue-side? Which ones track costs? What are your major cost categories (e.g. the top supply, labor, and distribution costs)?
- Which ones do you think can be changed versus which are static (i.e., they will only change slowly over the long-term)?
- How do you estimate the value of moving each of these metrics? How do you calculate it? What is a reasonable amount to improve it? How much impact would such an improvement have? Is that amount of benefit meaningful to your organization?
- Who in your organization is accountable for each of those metrics? For each, is there a single person or is accountability shared across many?
- Are each expected to persist or get better or worse over time?
- It may be a little early to get into the details of purchasing process, but at a high level: how does your organization buy solutions or products like this? Is the person who is on the hook for the metrics able to buy? What types of things do they buy today? Are buying decisions made by an individual or a committee? Do you buy directly from vendors or through a group purchasing organization? What are the typical buying decisions and processes (e.g. auto manufacturers require dozens of copies of a new part for twelve months to do four-season reliability testing.)

- For promising high $ areas, how do you solve them today and how effective are those solutions? (This gets us into Step #2.)

Invest a lot of your own time to experience the world from your buyer's point of view.

A few pitfalls to avoid

- Not every value pool is neatly measured. Value pools may be perceived to be larger or smaller by buyers than they actually are. Does that work to your advantage?
- In a B2C context (i.e. selling direct to the end user), adjustments to the above steps would have to be made—end users rarely have metrics they manage. You might have to be more hypothesis-driven in that setting. You still need to understand the source of value you're creating for them. Are you enriching the quality of their lives, replacing something they do today with something cheaper/faster/easier, or saving them time or money?
- Interview a lot of different types of buyers. Don't over-pivot on one person's voice.
- Identify a specific buyer. I hear a lot of young entrepreneurs saying things like "these events cost the health care system billions of dollars …" The health care system (at least in the US) is a combination of many stakeholders such as executives at large health insurance companies, hospital executives, independently-employed physicians who decide which tests in a hospital are ordered, employed nurses, hospital-based pharmacists and laboratory directors, and owners of local senior care facilities, to name a few. Who is absorbing the cost specifically and how?
- Don't discard a value pool just because buyers are currently defeated about the viability of solving it.
- Define the value pool in terms that your potential buyer would use; in ways that are independent of your solution. In mentoring student entrepreneurs, I often see them define a buyer problem in ways that assumes an interest in their technology or solution, such as: "farmers don't have access to lasers …". Farmers don't think in terms of lasers, they think in terms of the challenges of farming.
- Spend time learning and explaining the need. Don't hide behind words. Practice explaining the need to a five-year old. Explain the logic of the need and who owns it without resorting to technical terms or business jargon.

There are 4 steps … but you don't have to go in any particular order

In my current startup, we built our strategy by going through the following four steps in order, though we looped back several times along the way.

In contrast, at a prior company, we went out of order. There we had an existing product and were looking to apply it to other buyers and value pools. It was an e-learning product that had grown over the prior few years, but we didn't completely know why. So we started by determining why customers were buying from us, i.e. what our sources of advantage were

(Step 3). Only once we knew that, we then discussed new value pools (Step 1). From there, we then identified which of the current product "guardrails" we were comfortable maintaining or re-evaluating as we considered moving into using our product to address those new areas (Step 4).

Why do I need step 1 + 2 + 3 at all? Don't I just need to build something users will love?

If you start with the user and their needs (Step 4), it's important to do a loop back to the buyer (Step 1). In recent years, a few high-profile user-based tools, such as Snapchat, have biased us into a false premise that there's a generalizable approach to success that if you build something that users love, then, over time, revenue will follow. But without a buyer, you can't get revenue and most startups don't have enough funding to run for long without it.

Before you get started …

If you're going through a strategy development process for a company that already exists, it also helps a lot to have everyone aligned first on the mission and vision. This helps reinforce guardrails and focus the team on a long-term direction. Drafting a mission and vision as an early step for a startup can be challenging, so it may also help to come back to it once a first pass at the strategy is in place.

… And as you loop through

The best results come from iterating through the steps often and quickly. If you start with an existing technology or product (Step 2), try to develop early insights on potential buyers and their needs (Step 1). Anchoring too long on one step without iterating through the others may bias you towards believing a solution exists to thread all four steps when such a solution may not exist.

Step #2: What's Our Unique Approach to Unlock the Value Pool?

This is Step 2 of "4 Steps to Develop a Strategy", focused on identifying the root causes of a buyer's pain point, determining why it hasn't been solved already, and outlining our approach/technology to do so.

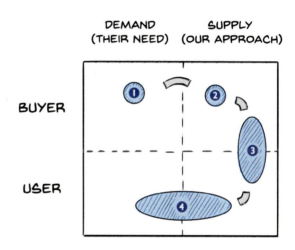

(2a) List out all the root causes of the high $ value pool

This step typically follows Step 1 (the process of identifying a buyer and value pool).

This step should not be super difficult. Ideally there are many publications on the top drivers of the pain point we can reference and by citing them, everyone will nod their heads in agreement. Be concerned if it's too difficult; while we should do our own research into the root causes of the value pool we identify, we don't want to have to spend time in a sales meeting educating our potential customers about this.

Interviews again are a valuable tool
At one point in my career, I investigated building a product that would help reduce patient falls in a hospital. I decided not to pursue it and partly for that reason, it makes a good case study.

For Step 1, I talked to *buyers* about how they measure the cost of falls and how much value they see in a further reduction. I also asked them the mechanisms they have seen effective for fall reduction and which ones they use, or are considering using, today.

I talked to the prospective *users* of such a solution—in this example, physicians, nurses, and nurse assistants. In my experience, offering people a gift card for thirty minutes of their time for an expert interview will allow you to hear the voice from the front lines—and it is always well worth it. In any case, I asked nurses what the root cause of patient falls were.

At this point, our team began to imagine solutions based on what we learned about the main cause of falls (e.g. elderly people getting up to go to the bathroom) and how they were currently prevented (e.g. checking in on patients regularly). One solution the team came up with was an alert for the nurse when the patients' weight is no longer present on their bed.

Note we're not looking to invent a product here, but rather to identify a solution approach (also known as a product strategy or value proposition) that a product could be built around. In this example, a scale under the bed could be a solution, but not a "product" yet. We don't know what the users' needs are and so we don't know yet what product features would be needed to have them use it.

I've also done surveys. In this case, surveying 300 nurses to find out the root causes they see in patient falls would tell us a lot. The result of that work would be something we can deploy as part of our marketing materials later on. All you need are an email list and the ability to offer a $15 Amazon gift card for a few minutes of their time. You may find it best to do your research first so you can ask meaningful, informed, and hypothesis-driven questions in a survey.

Whether you talk to potential customers individually, in groups, in person, or by phone matters less than the fact you are talking to them. As Steve Blank (the "godfather" of the Lean Startup methodology) says, "there are no facts inside your building, so get the heck outside."

The interview questions for a prospective buyer or user in this step are:

- Are you able to solve this value pool today? How effective are current solutions? What is the cost of those solutions? (Especially where there is a direct competitor, you will have to gauge your cost comparison to those alternative solutions.)
- What is preventing current solutions from being existing or being effective? Why are you still stuck with this need? Have you not been compelled to try to address it? Or have you tried many approaches and none have worked? Are you trying any actively now?
- How well do you think some new method of solving this problem will work? Could you imagine it solving the problem on its own?
- What is your day like? What are the other things you're worried about?
- Even if a high ROI solution to this problem existed, are there so many other firefights going on that it might not be urgent enough for you to act?

(2b) Determine why the value pool isn't being solved today: Are there major root causes not being addressed? Or are current approaches just not effective?

The value of finding unaddressed root causes

This is where you look for Blue Ocean—value pool solution approaches that don't exist today. Other companies may know the value pools (as discussed in Step #1), but the current competitors are likely focusing in on solving one or two of the root causes and solutions to the value pool. Are there any root causes that are being overlooked today? If so, coupled with a unique product approach, this is where you can do something different and impact your customers' value pools in a way that's complementary to what they're already doing.

Strategy at its core is carving out divergent solutions and approaches. Ivan M. Arreguín-Toft's analysis in "How the Weak Win Wars" shows that taking a divergent strategy allows the smaller player to win two-thirds of the time. But taking a strategy similar to an incumbent's wins only one-fifth of the time.

There are three ways to be different: choosing an over-looked buyer, choosing a value pool / pain point for that customer that no one else has noticed, and, finally, choosing a novel approach to solve that pain point.

What root causes have others overlooked so far? They are often in plain sight

Other entrepreneurs may know the high $ value pools (even if they ignore them). But identifying the root causes with front-line observation and then brainstorming new ways to address any present-but-not-yet-served root causes is where unique ideas come to light.

It's not the buyers' or users' jobs to articulate what the problems are or where current solutions don't work and why. But they can tell you what they are happy with today and where major points of frustration are, especially if you focus them on a particular part of their day or work, such as identifying and preventing patient falls.

In the patient falls example, we asked the user (i.e. the nurse) to walk us through how they worked with patients. How much is fall prevention on their mind? Do they spend a lot of time running to check on patients?

You will hear their real concerns and attitudes and they will help you correct misconceptions you may have. This will help you better zero in on new solutions that are optimized to their context. More effective still may be to ask patients who fell what the care team could have done to avoid the event.

Observing users in real life can allow you to see points of wasted time and effort, sources of frustration, missed opportunities, and overlooked causes and solutions. I love to do that anthropological research in person… but while I can get twenty people on the phone, who will volunteer to let me watch in their homes and offices? A colleague of mine launched a new venture within a company who had many existing customers. In that situation, he used those relationships to observe users in real life. For me, I have found phone interviews to work well.

(2c) Choose a method of unlocking the value pool—ideally one that's based on a unique technology or insight

If there are many competitors already providing solutions to the buyer's need/value pool similar to the one you are considering, you have to have a strong belief you can build yours uniquely enough to win a certain customer segment. Don't immediately worry about competitors: having competitors is validation of the need you identified. Instead focus on differentiating against those competitors.

Where there are existing players, opportunities can still be attractive if you can avoid becoming a commodity. In the chart below, you can see the relative attractiveness of a strategy based on the differentiation to incumbents in (1) choosing a buyer/value pool and (2) a method of unlocking that value pool.

For (2), if there are many competitors or in-house solutions addressing a value pool, but doing so in dissimilar ways as your solution, you can still be successful. I'll warn you that potential buyers may react with "well, we're already doing so much in this area, let's see how those initiatives do before we start up a new one."

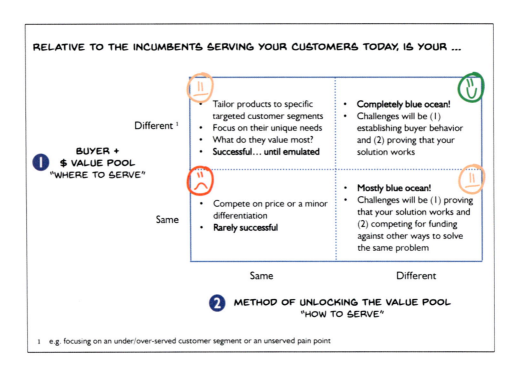

When evaluating your point of differentiation relative to existing players ("the method of unlocking value pool"), make sure it is fully grounded in how you serve that value pool. Do not evaluate on some immaterial product feature.

What is the unique technology or analytics/data that you are bringing to the solution? If you don't have a clear answer, why wasn't your solution already built years ago by someone else? The unique technology or analytical core should become a source of advantage that will deter copycats and enable you to find a unique voice in a crowded field of competitors. More on that in the next section.

Do a quick investigation into the types of companies that have solutions similar to yours. Talk to a leader who has started such a company in the past. What are the revenue multiples for an acquisition of such a company? Typically, software-as-a-service companies can reach 5-10x revenue multiples; this is high enough to attract engineers with stock options and investors. Consulting solutions, in contrast, are typically acquired at about 1x revenue. I was working recently with a startup that had a unique polymer for textiles; when we discovered the typical revenue multiples for such companies is 1x, it caused us to rethink the types of investment we might make. Lower multiples mean less likelihood of attracting investors and are also typically indicative of less innovative spaces with limited value creation potential.

A pitfall to avoid

- Don't hide behind words. Practice explaining the technology / fundamentals of your approach to a five-year old. Avoid using any technical terms or business jargon.

Step #3: Why Us? Why Can't Two Kids in a Dorm Room Build This?

This is Step 3 of "4 Steps to Develop a Strategy", focused on understanding why we're the company or team that can uniquely solve the buyer's pain point. In short, we need an ironclad answer to, "Why can't two kids in a dorm room build this? What are our super-powers?"

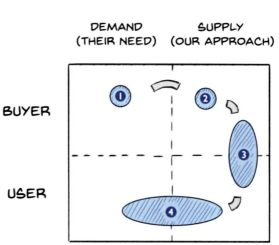

(3a) List out the unique assets + expertise we have that makes us the best team to implement this new method of unlocking our chosen value pool (i.e. our sources of advantage)

What do we as a team do uniquely well? What skills, knowledge, or insights must we really leverage if we will give ourselves the best chance of building something great? What are our "super-powers"?

At the early stage of identifying a problem to solve and building a product, you may not have a specific solution in mind. Nonetheless, you should at least have some idea of the core competencies you can bring to any problem and be able to articulate why those competencies will be the cornerstone of a viable solution.

What are the technical insights or tools we have built (or see a clear path to build) that are beyond what others are seeing today? Can we inject them into the solution for a value pool?

What will allow us to help our customers accomplish something 2-, 3-, 5-, or 10-times faster, cheaper, or better than they otherwise could?

What are the insights we have about what creates value for our users and buyers that others are not adhering to? For example, in my current company, a relentless focus on teeing up specific actions for users to take versus just showing them data in a dashboard was such a source of advantage for us that we rallied around it constantly. It defined us and our product. It was an insight that, when built into the culture of the company, became a consistent source of advantage.

If anyone can do it or easily copy it, how will we develop and maintain differentiated solution?

Merge a value pool (customer need) with what you do uniquely well and you're on a good path. Jeff Bezos, Amazon's CEO, said in a 2009 *Fast Company* interview, "There are two ways to extend a business. Take inventory of what you're good at and extend out from your skills. Or determine what your customers need and work backward even if it requires learning new skills." Magic also happens if you can do both.

What we're talking about here are sources of competitive advantage. You can also think of them as your super-powers.

Competitive advantages don't last as long as they used to. Thirty-year advantages in the 1970s may have been typical, but a company may only be able to get five to ten years out of an advantage today.

In one of my prior companies, we built an e-learning platform for doctors and nurses. We had illustrators, learning designers, engineers, clinicians, copywriters, assessment question writers, statisticians, and many others who worked together to create hard-hitting content. That collection of individuals, working within a process that we had developed over the prior years was a definite source of advantage. Our competitors may have been able to mimic some of our outputs but it would have taken years for them to recreate the engine we had put together.

Why can't two kids in a dorm room do this? What are our sources of advantage?
You need to have a good answer to the question of why you are uniquely situated to build the solution. Because if that answer isn't strong, you're probably underestimating the challenges.

Know your strengths and play to them. Generally speaking, for example, 35-year-old corporate executives don't break into professional baseball.

KNOW YOUR STRENGTHS AND PLAY TO THEM.
GENERALLY SPEAKING, FOR EXAMPLE, 35-YEAR-OLD
CORPORATE EXECUTIVES DON'T BREAK INTO
PROFESSIONAL BASEBALL.

strategist.blog

The same is true of a startup. If you can't articulate and quantify why you are uniquely the right set of people to tackle a particular problem, then you should at least ask yourself why hasn't somebody else solved it?

What privileged information do you have about your buyers and their needs? What do you know about your users and how they experience the world? Do you have a unique technology?

As a new company, consider what personal strengths the founding team has, such as industry knowledge, an ability to operate with high mobility (i.e. fast-product-feedback-loops), analytics horsepower, unique customer insights, sales connections into the customer base, or access to founding capital. Compare these to strengths a startup most likely doesn't have, though incumbent competitors often do: strong brand recognition, at-scale engineering and marketing teams, distribution relationships, and global scale such as in hiring employees and buying supplies.

All organizations have potential sources of competitive advantage.

As a company grows into multiple products, these things we do uniquely well become standards that apply in strategies at all levels of the company. The detailed activities and decisions of how those sources of advantage are deployed (covered in Step #4) will vary by product but these pillars remain consistent. P&G refers to them as "reinforcing rods" that link all parts of an organization together.

Personally, I am interested in building companies where analytics is (or could become) a source of advantage. This is because a unique data feed from your customers can create a flywheel of new insights, innovation, and growth—which then allows your competitive advantages to last much longer.

In the words of Peter Drucker, "put yourself where your strengths can produce results… waste as little effort as possible on improving areas of low competence."

Strategic jiujitsu: Lessons from Southwest Airlines, Western Europe, and the Simpsons

Can you *create* a source of advantage by inverting what appears to be a barrier to entry?

Southwest Airlines gives us a great case study here. In the 1970s, all the incumbent major airlines had purchased the rights to the gates of the major airports, thus preventing new airlines from flying out of them.

Conceivably, anyone could buy planes and hire grounds crew, but there were no gates available to dock those planes at the major airports. However, this approach had also caused those incumbent airlines to abandon gates at smaller airports. By buying the rights to those gates, Southwest was able to overcome a major barrier to entry and then leveraged the positive aspect of those assets (e.g. faster gate turnaround time) to build a unique solution. How's that for some strategic jiujitsu?

The Western European countries in the 1400s give us an example. Trade between Europe and the East was very profitable but Venice and other Eastern European cities had a geographical advantage and were already incumbents. England, Portugal, Spain, and the Netherlands were locked out of owning a part of the eastern-directed trade routes so they instead looked west. By doing so, they found the Americas, which, in the following centuries, became a far greater source of imperial power and wealth.

As another example, in the companies I've helped build, we've always sold to hospitals. There are so many barriers to entry when doing so: you need to really understand their complex workflows, have connections already to hospital leadership to avoid having to rely on cold calls, be able to weather and navigate very long sales cycles, and have technology platforms that are HIPAA-compliant, for example. But by recognizing these barriers and by having a clever path around them (e.g. by having solved these challenges many times before as a team, we had a playbook), we've been able to turn this barrier into an advantage.

One final example of strategic jiujitsu comes from The Simpsons on Christmas Eve ("Twelve glasses of water", Season 9, Episode 10). Bart, upon finishing drinking a lot of water: "Twelve glasses of water. That'll wake me up nice and early and I'll have a big head start on opening presents. Pure genius." Lisa replies, "You didn't invent that, Bart. The Indians used to drink water to wake up early for their attack." Though Bart gets the last word: "it's always about the Indians, isn't it, Lise?" Anyway, that's strategy: taking something that appears to be working against you (e.g. waking up in the middle of the night to go to the bathroom) and finding a use case of it that works to your advantage.

Why is it important to know what your super-powers are and to build off of them?

Whenever you are considering a new product, or feature for an existing product, a core question in determining if/when/and how to build it should be, "does this leverage and reflect our super-powers?" Because if not, are we just going to be a me-too player if we build it? And if we apply our super-power problem-solving to it, can any new feature be made better and continually reinforce our overall differentiation?

If you're an established company looking to grow

If you're a company who already has a core product that is now looking to grow into new customer segments, you need to identify a new value pool and then determine if the existing product/capabilities/advantages can be applied to unlock that value pool.

In my prior company, where I led our strategy team, we wanted to determine other areas to take our e-learning product. We searched for different buyers and/or value pools and found many that were compelling. For example, we had an e-learning platform and a lot of expertise in developing medical content. Let's return to the value pool discussed in Step #2, patient fall prevention. The question at hand was: is e-learning an effective solution to the root causes of falls? It turned out, after talking with buyers and users, that most hospitals were putting protocols in place to avoid falls; training clinicians to improve their judgment in order to do so wasn't considered to be a compelling solution.

In an established company, start by determining what's driving your profits today. What do you do uniquely well? Why are customers paying you?

It is your sources of competitive advantage that lead to profits.

What customer segments are most profitable? What products? Why? The advantages may be market-based (i.e. you chose a great place to be in), your own (your product is uniquely valuable), or both. Those are the areas you want to build on—to leverage your strengths to create new areas of value while reinforcing the strengths your current business is built on. An easy way is to ask your buyers and users what they find most valuable.

Make sure you really investigate though. I've seen companies misread these tea leaves far too often. Companies that operate in one very specific space and have a well-known brand in that space tend to assume that they're good at branding. Companies that have done small roll-up acquisitions in a specific space assume that they're good at M&A. Companies with a specific product that is profitable tend to then assume they are good at growth and low-cost operations as generalizable competencies, for example. It's probably not so. What you need to understand are the specific series of steps you take to provide your product to your customer today that others cannot emulate.

"The most robust competitive positions often cumulate from many activities," writes Michael Porter, because a coherent collection is harder to mimic.

True sources of advantage are ones you can invest in and they become stronger over time. As you increase their value, you can then leverage them for more products, which further strengthens them.

(3b) Identify the trends in the macro environment that our method can tap into

No one can predict the future and no strategy should require you to do so. Your strategy should hold strong as the future unfolds in unexpected ways.

While surprises can appear, there are always macro trends that move slowly and if you're tapping into them, your odds of success are much higher. Likewise, your odds of becoming extinct are high if you are fighting against these trends.

Cisco is a great example. To understand its enormous success in the 1990s, we need to observe the trends it was fortunate to ride. Cisco started by creating super-fast routers that build clever code into the chips in its router. None of the other players could replicate it because it codified the skill of its nimble team of experts into software. Riding this first trend of hardware to software allowed Cisco to overcome the size advantages of IBM and AT&T.

Cisco was well-placed for the rise of corporate networks when companies went on major spending sprees to implement internet connectivity in their buildings. And then they positioned themselves a few years later for the public internet when it created a similar need for networks in people's houses.

Satya Nadella became CEO of Microsoft because, in his prior role there, he saw the potential of the cloud market and dedicated all of his team's time and resources into developing Microsoft's early services there. The business grew and his reputation along with it.

strategist.blog

McKinsey's research shows that about 40% of a company's success, on average, is determined solely by the industry that it is in.

What will the world look like in 10-20 years and how will we be a leader in it?
Questions to ask here include:

- What are the major trends emerging now related to the product space we're in? What are the new analytics tools everyone is talking about? The new user interface technologies? The newly emerging industry trends that industry analysts write about? How can we connect ourselves to any or all of these?
- Without trying to predict the future, what are some views on how it may unfold? Where will new value pools emerge? How will competitive advantages change over time?
- Where will new pools of surplus emerge? Where will new competitive threats emerge? Interview experts to learn more. Hold a management workshop to explore/add to trends.
- Look for areas of privileged information or insight. What do we know/see that competitors don't?
- Research new technologies and imagine likelihood/impact of marginal producers as new entrants.
- How will the market change over five years? What are frontier/early adopter/they-may-be-the-future customers doing (e.g. in China)?
- Where are the greatest global investments and growth likely to be? What are the underlying factors of our historical growth, how directly have they driven our growth, and where will those evolve?
- How do we position ourselves in front of these market trend tailwinds versus trying to mitigate their negative effect?

Identifying trends is a separate topic from identifying your sources of advantage. But they both work together to create a north star: go in the direction where both your strengths and the prevailing winds will most work to your benefit.

Step #4: How Will We Engage and Delight Our Users?

This is Step 4 of "4 Steps to Develop a Strategy", focused on finding power users who have already been compelled to find some solution to a need they have. Can we productize some version of it to serve other users while addressing the buyer's pain point in the same product?

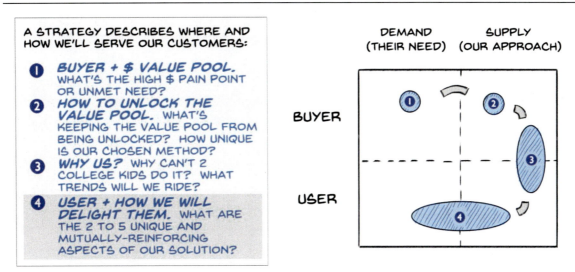

There's a difference between a strategy and a product definition. This step is not about building a product (that has to be an iterative process with actual users over time), but rather about defining the few pillars of the product that put both a direction and guardrails on your product development.

Determining who your users are is a first step. The next step is knowing your users well enough to know the jobs they are struggling to accomplish. How are they being under- or over-served by other products they use: not only competitive products, but all products and services they interact with?

This final step in creating a strategy is to tie the first three steps together and define how we will win over users with the core pillars of a product offering. To recap, building on the four-part framework above, assuming we moved in order, at this point from the prior three steps we ideally have a draft of these steps completed:

1) Find a high $ pain point that keeps someone awake at night
   a. Identify a buyer
   b. Identify a high $ value pool
2) What's stopping the pain point from being addressed today? What are the root causes of it? Which ones haven't been addressed? Which ones could benefit from a novel approach?
   a. List out all the root causes of the high $ value pool
   b. Determine why the value pool isn't being solved today: Are there major root causes not being addressed? Or are current approaches just not effective?
   c. Choose a method of unlocking the value pool—ideally one that's based on a unique technology or insight
3) Why us? Have an ironclad answer to: "Why can't two kids in a dorm room build this? What are our superpowers?"
   a. List out the unique assets + expertise we have that makes us the best team to implement this new method of unlocking our chosen value pool (i.e. our sources of advantage)
   b. Identify the trends in the macro environment that our method can tap into
4) What do our users (who are not our buyers) want? The goal in this step is to not invent a solution, but rather to find power users who have cobbled one together and productize it

I should add… no new business can nail these criteria as they get started. Some of them have to be figured out over time. But by articulating them to this point, we have at least identified the strength of an opportunity and highlighted many of the major risks.

Why do we need Step 4 at all? Isn't it enough to have identified a value pool?
Whatever value pool you identify, you should be aware that the market will be flooded with companies claiming to solve it. You can differentiate based on ROI case studies (when you get them) and a focus on a unique root cause … but more valuably, based on a focus on a unique user and a unique way of serving that user. Win over the user and the buyer will follow.

Software as a Service (SaaS) companies are realizing that contract renewals are determined in the first few weeks of deployment: if users are engaged and adopt quickly, renewals two or three years later are already on a strong path.

While delighting your users won't fully be solved in your strategy, the rough guideline for accomplishing it has to start with the strategy. A focus on the buyer is not enough. We now turn to the user.

(4a) Identify our users. Our buyers are not our users.

My colleagues and I kicked off our most recent startup about 18 months ago. We knew our "buyers" very well, having served Chief Nursing Officers in hospitals for many years. We scoped out and pitched a product to them that we believed would solve one of their most pressing needs, the need to engage and retain their clinical workforce.

We also knew our "users": nurse managers in those hospitals. We knew that nurse managers had a very difficult role and designed a product approach based on dozens of hours of discussion and feedback with those managers, as any good Lean Startup would do.

We also knew that buyers wouldn't buy our product if they didn't truly believe that the users would use it, so there was natural alignment there. But what I have consistently been surprised by in the course of the past months is how different the two stakeholders' needs are and how difficult it is to be a startup that is trying to thread the needle between them both.

A large number of our product and strategy discussions have been around what to build, how to organize what we are building, and how to message it. In so many discussions, the question has come down to: should we build for (and message to) the buyer or the user? And if we want to balance both, how do we best do it? Which one matters more for sales? For product adoption? For impact?

I don't profess to have a perfect generalizable solution to the challenge. I simply raise the distinction because realizing that we had multiple stakeholders and part of the magic of our product is to unite them both has helped us.

Terms like "Product-Market Fit" are ubiquitous and are a good example that we often don't disentangle buyers and users.

In our startup, we evaluate our "Product-Buyer Fit" and "Product-User Fit" separately, for example.

Buyers are not users… even when they're the same person.
If they are the same person, they are still different stakeholders. Too often, strategists merge buyers and users into "customer" and they lose insight because of it. Buyers and users have different goals and pain points.

For example, how many times have you (as a buyer) bought a plane ticket and chosen the cheapest one?   Then weeks later when you (as a user) are waiting in long lines, sitting in a cramped middle seat, and suffering through delays and cancellations… and cursing the earlier version of yourself for being such a cheapskate?

When you are serving the user, delight them with what they care about (e.g. how easy your product is to use); that's a great way to have them buy from you again. But don't distract the buyer with messages about what only the user values.

BUYERS AND USERS ARE DIFFERENT STAKEHOLDERS

strategist.blog

In a B2B context/enterprise sale, buyers and users are decidedly different. In the 1990s and 2000s, Microsoft and Blackberry could gain a lot of scale selling to companies because they knew how to win over the buyer, the Chief Technology Officer (CTO). CTOs want a cost-effective product that serves a set of basic needs, that is easy to maintain, and that doesn't have security issues. CTOs did not worry too much about user preferences. In contrast, Apple sold to users. Apple built a great experience for them and, over time, users demanded support for their products from their CTOs. CTOs now typically support both Apple and Microsoft platforms. The same thing is playing out (ten years later) with Electronic Medical Record Systems in hospitals. Hospital CTOs bought a solution that met basic buyer needs, but the users (physicians and nurses) are demanding solutions that are much easier to use and more clinically informed.

Buyers and users are different even in a B2C context

All advertising-based internet companies (such as Google or Facebook) have corporations as their buyers and offer their unique services (such as internet searches, maps, or email) for free to deliver the buyers' ads to them. Or for a simpler example, parents buy cereal (based on their preferences) for their kids to eat (who will do so based on their own set of criteria).

P&G has a motto that it communicates to all employees: "Win the two most important moments of truth". The first moment of truth is when the customer experiences the product, such as Tide detergent, in the store. Is it in stock? Easy to find? Does the packaging support the brand's message? The second moment is when the customer experiences the product at home. Is the detergent's fragrance enjoyable? Are their whites whiter? P&G doesn't use the term buyer and user when talking about their customers … but the idea is the same.

(4b) Determine the two to five unique and pivotal decisions that will define our solution—and will delight our users

Our chosen method for addressing the value pool is only the start. Here we need to weave in the user. How can we delight them while impacting the buyer's value pool? How will we create raving fans?

These have to be directly connected to our sources of advantage as well. In Southwest Airlines' case study, for example, their value pool and source of advantage focused them on serving short distance travelers from smaller, more suburban airports. Therefore, it would have been out of synch for them to choose first-class dining or multiple business class seating hierarchies in how they served their user. From their value pool and source of advantage, you can clearly draw a direct path to being a lower cost and more agile company across the board.

Our goal is to develop the two to five unique and pivotal decisions that define our solution. Determining what they are is perhaps the hardest part of developing a strategy. Often, when starting on a new product, you don't know, because it requires a working knowledge of the user and what they value. But it's important to build a perspective and evolve it.

These decisions will allow us to best serve our chosen buyers and users, leverage our sources of advantage, and align us with the larger trends. These decisions should be internally consistent and mutually-reinforcing.

For example, with a company I was a part of, we believed that generating insights from a particular data source would be one of the core product attributes that would define our solution. Over time, we discovered that component of our product wasn't as important to our users—so we demoted it and promoted other decisions. So, while all Four Steps of a strategy are connected and will evolve, this section needs a strawman that gets re-evaluated often, especially in the early days.

Interviews are still a valuable tool
We need to talk to potential users about what product would be valuable for them, centered on the chosen method. Resist the urge to jump into a specific product solution. And resist the urge to frame the problem in terms of the buyers. If we go to nurses and say, "your CEO wants to accomplish this and here's a product we're working on that can help do that", the odds are they will say, "Great! Another thing for me to do that's pushed on me by the administration! Don't they understand how busy I am and how I have no time to do every new thing they come up with?"

What you have to do is talk to the users about their needs and areas of friction and build your product and story to them around where they are.

The interview questions in this step are:

- What is a typical day like for you? Document the blocks of time they spend doing tasks and what tools they use.

- For example, are they on email for two hours every day, such as ten to noon? Are they walking around talking to people? In meetings? On phone calls? Where and what tools are they in front of during these times?
- What are your main goals? What jobs are you trying to accomplish? Can a new solution help them with the entire task?
    - Look for tasks where you can imagine a product solving a complete need. If their daily goal is to assemble, review, and approve expense reports, a tool that helps them upload expense reports may go unused—they still need to keep their current tools and existing workflow to complete the task.
- Do you care about what the buyers care about (i.e. the value pool)?
- What are your greatest areas of frustration? Need? Friction? For example, that there is no free time in the day and they are spending a lot of time on low-value activities.
- When was the last time you solved this problem? If you hadn't chosen the solution you did, what else would you have done?
    - What is the single most critical job that the user is trying to accomplish that your product can fulfill? Blackberry phones were popular for many years because they were the best devices to read and send emails; other devices did games, internet, and maps better, but couldn't compete with Blackberries until they improved their email experience. Do one important job well. Don't bet a product on doing many small jobs well.

Asking this last question gets to "the jobs to be done" mindset, a way of structuring user behavior that Clayton Christensen popularized.

You need to accomplish a job the user is already trying to solve

Let me be clear: no user will use your product unless it helps them solve a problem or accomplish a critical job they are trying to solve (even if it solves a buyer's problem and the buyer is their boss). To get product usage, you need a user's internal triggers to fire and then you want to be the reaction they have to that trigger firing. You cannot create usage by giving people a product and saying it does something new that they are not trying to do. Amazon on a cellphone does this for many people: whenever they think they need to buy something, it's easier to open their phone and buy it than it is to write it down on a shopping list and buy it later in a store. The internal trigger fires and Amazon is the brain's go to response.

Don't build two loosely joined products here—one that solves the buyer's need and another for the user. Focus on doing one thing well. The magic is threading the needle between the users' and the buyers' needs.

You don't want to invent something new…

Building companies and products should almost always be innovation, not invention. Inventions are riskier and can take years to get right. Innovation is the process of taking something that already invented and applying a business model and strategy around it.

I have observed colleagues take the invention path. They imagine a solution to a need but have to first build the core components of that solution from the ground up.

A rubric for me is: If you can imagine getting a patent for the product that emerges from your solution, or any core part of it (and you haven't already built it and proven it works). then your solution is an invention, not an innovation.

Software and analytics solutions require no de novo invention; if you know how to use the tools, you will carve out a working solution. There is no risk it will take years to prove that something works. One reason there have been so many successful software and web-based companies over the past twenty years is that building a software product has no risk that the product won't function; the only risk is finding the right version of it that will best meet customers' needs. Perhaps innovative companies like Tesla and Apple would not exist if their founders had followed the advice of avoiding invention. But my goals for a startup are different: to get a product to market in six months, to be revenue-generating in a year, and to be profitable in twenty-four months.

The science fiction writer William Gibson (author of *Neuromancer*) has said, "The future is already here; it's just not very evenly distributed."

Find the "power users" out there and ask them what solutions they have cobbled together for themselves. Then productize that.

Power users are the most forward-thinking of your user base. They are often the most tech savvy, may have multiple cross-disciplinary degrees, and/or may have worked in another industry. Use LinkedIn to find people who meet that profile and interview them.

Look at what they've built themselves. If users have a real need, they're not going to sit still while waiting for someone else to solve it.

Before Apple made a PC available to the masses, technophiles in the 1970s were cobbling home computers together in their garages. Before Tesla made electric cars commercially viable, auto enthusiasts had built early versions. In corporate headquarters everywhere, power users have complex Excel spreadsheets that help them solve business needs.

The odds are that users are not immediately solving a problem aligned with a buyers' value pool. But aligning them to win over both in a single product is where you should focus your efforts.

Find the smallest prototype of the product/solution that will fit both buyer and users' needs

This is often called the "Minimal Viable Product" (MVP) in the lean startup vernacular. I prefer the term "prototype"; MVP includes the word "product" which already plants the idea that it has to be something real. Prototype, on the other hand, conjures the right image for me: something duct-taped together in an afternoon. It doesn't matter how rudimentary or unscalable it is. Its goal is to help you learn about what your buyers and users need and want.

If yours is an analytics company, could you imagine some early, viable version of the solution being built in Microsoft Excel? You might not actually build it that way, but if you can imagine it, you can then imagine how you could build a working version of your product in six months. On the flip side, do you need massive data to get started, which you don't have? Or do you need to invent something that doesn't exist today just to get started? If the latter, that would be a warning flag for me.

I know entrepreneurs who are willing to gamble on months of major innovation. I'm not one. In my experience, this is a main differentiator between successful startups and unsuccessful ones. It's risky to go through two to three years of no-revenue de novo innovation and only then try to build a commercial product.

The lynchpin to whether your company and product will take off is whether your users will adopt the product

A topic we'll come back to later is how to drive daily usage. Daily usage occurs when you are solving continuous headaches for your users. Monthly usage often occurs when you're solving larger, more important issues that, by definition, won't appear as often. Can your product solve both under a seamless UI? LinkedIn does it by connecting both daily pulse of updates from your professional colleagues with the higher-ROI product of connecting you to a new job every few years.

Savvy investors will probably push you on this part of your strategy when you are fundraising. Getting users to use something new or otherwise change behavior is notoriously difficult. The trick is to find tasks they do today and make them easier or automate them. Then, building on that, you can add in other elements to the product once you have their attention.

You want your product to be part of real-time tasks or processes that the user already has, because creating new behaviors is hard. For example, if your user is already spending hours on email, can you get your product to fit inside of their inbox somehow? These insights will help you figure out how to fit your product into their lives without disrupting their core activities. What are the entire tasks they are doing today that you can help them do 2-5x faster, 2-5x more efficiently, 2-5x more enjoyably, or simply 2-5x more of?

The art is building a product that solves both the user's daily headaches and impacts the buyer's long-term value pool.

Keep looping through the "4 Steps to Develop a Strategy." You don't have to go in order

You will need to loop back through all of the steps, perhaps multiple times. It's about impossible to go through the Four Steps in order, linearly, with one pass, and emerge victoriously.

One approach is to start with a unique solution based on products your company already has and then look for value pools to apply it to. Pharmaceutical companies do this all the time:

they discover a new molecular drug and then find it has a side effect which happens to solve another marketable need. Whichever direction you go through the list, you have to iterate. Strategy is the art of keeping these plates spinning while you find the best combination.

As you loop through, nuances will emerge. For example, once you have a draft of the Four Steps and you go back to test it out with buyers and users in another round of interviews, you can ask: why can't the incumbents develop this? Can they easily extend from their current product into this new area?

Focusing on a buyer, value pool, and user will give you a clear path to creating unique value

For a startup, focus is the answer. Focus on a specific buyer segment/industry, a specific value pool, and a specific user. A startup can then structure the challenge that those buyers/users are facing to develop a product built around that structure that makes the greatest possible impact on the value pool.

In a public example, Olay, the P&G skin care product, re-launched in 2000 with the tagline that Olay fought "the seven signs of aging". By doing so, Olay took a buyer's complete value pool when all of their competitors only focused on wrinkles. They thus positioned Olay to have a far greater impact than anyone else could.

Step #4 is an especially iterative process that takes time.

A pitfall to avoid

- Don't zero-in and commit to a path too quickly. If you are anchoring on a value pool (Step 1), investigate many potential root causes and solutions. If you are anchoring on a technology (Step 2), investigate many potential buyers and value pools. It's not uncommon for teams to spend months building out a solution on one path and realize it won't work; if you already have a set of alternatives, pivoting, if needed, will be far more efficient.

Why Strategy and Analytics? Why, Together, are They Important?

Close Your Eyes and Imagine a Strategy. Let Me Guess: Got Nothing?

Close your eyes for a minute and imagine a strategy.

Are you imagining a simple, specific document you refer to for helpful guidance that summarizes your company's north star?

Or are you imagining absolutely nothing?

Don't blame yourself. In Michael Porter's books, or anywhere else, I haven't been able to find many examples of what a strategy should look like.

Here's a proposal: open any book on strategy and go to the Index. Lookup "Strategy, an example of". Find anything?

STRATEGIC M...
STRATEGY:
 ART OF, 112
 BIG MOVES AS GOOD 166-170
 BOTTOM-UP, 21
 COMPANY-WIDE, 32
 COMPETITIVE ADVANTAGE AND, 165-166
 DEVELOPMENT OF, 34
 EXAMPLE OF, ??????
 FAILURES OF, 67
 IMPROVEMENT PROCESS, 2
 ... PROCESS, 13-15, 60, 177

TYPICAL INDEX FOR A BOOK ON STRATEGY

strategist.blog

The "4 Steps to Develop a Strategy" outline the four major components that a good corporate strategy needs:

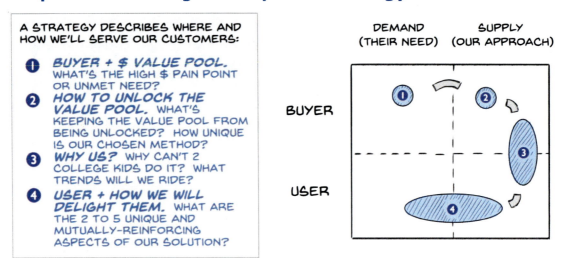

A strategy could cover these four components in ten to twenty sentences.

Why not a 200-page plan? Because if every one of your employees can't remember the strategy and don't know how to use it to prioritize their day, what good is it? A strategy needs to be specific enough to be helpful, but short enough to be memorable. It should be something that everyone can refer to. Companies often either do too little strategic thinking and/or create too much "strategic material". Either way, they avoid the hard work of these 4 Steps.

Here's my best guess at Southwest Airlines' strategy circa the 1970s (it has changed little since)

Southwest Airlines' Strategy

1. **Buyer + $ value pool.** What's the high $ pain point or unmet need?
   - Anyone who travels distances that take 4-8 hours by car (e.g. over-served by major airlines) who want a faster and similarly low-cost alternative. Need will only grow (unless high-speed rails take off).
2. **How to unlock the $ value pool.** What's keeping the value pool from being unlocked? How unique is our chosen method?
   - When an existing airline attempts a short-hop flight, the airports they fly into (the major urban hubs) take a long time for passengers to get to. And it takes a long time to park, get through security, and board—so the total door-to-door time is too long. You might as well drive the whole way.

We'll specifically choose hubs and processes with the explicit goal of shortening that time as much as possible.

❸ Why us? What are our sources of advantage? What trends will we ride?

- Founding team's deep knowledge of what is required to build and operate an airline
- The insight that all the major airlines have purchased the rights to gates of all major airports, thus locking new airlines from flying into them. However, this has also caused those incumbents to ignore gates at smaller suburban airports. By buying the rights to those gates, Southwest can overcome this barrier to entry. This means Southwest can reduce door-to-door travel time for passengers but also limits the ability to transfer passengers between other airlines.
- Unique customer insights about sources of unmet customer needs
- The existing airlines are stuck in their long-haul models and can't reorganize to challenge us serving customers on these types of trips.
- Over time, scale, as a dedication to building our approach into all areas of our delivery systems will make it impossible for anyone to mimic us.
- There is a big trend emerging in airline de-regulation. For example, profitability now has to be earned but the existing airlines have been guaranteed profits under regulation.

❹ User + how we will delight them. What are the two to five unique and pivotal decisions that will define our solution?

- Limited passenger services
    i. Such as no first class; no frequent flier miles; open seating/first-come-first-on; passengers cleaning up after themselves to speed up gate turnarounds; no meals
- Be lowest cost
    i. Such as flying one aircraft type, the 737; thus, also not needing to train and certify pilots on other aircraft; No travel agents or 3rd party travel websites—you can only book with the airline thus avoiding royalty fees.
- Highly agile and invested grounds and air crew
    i. Such as personality-infused pre-flight safety presentations; employee stock ownership; ground and flight crews well compensated; crews allowed to join unions; crews empowered on any safety issue. Let employees be our "eyes and ears" for new ways to continually improve our service to customers.

Every employee can understand this and can apply it to decisions they make day-to-day. Even though it (or a variant of it) should be shared across the company, it should be specific enough to be confidential.

Here's my guess at Fitbit's strategy circa 2015:

Fitbit's Strategy

1 Buyer + $ value pool. What's the high $ pain point or unmet need?

- Regular people looking to do more exercise. They see regular exercise as a way to increase the years and quality of their life.

2 Ways to unlock the $ value pool. What's keeping the value pool from being unlocked? How unique is our chosen method?

- Instead of focusing on different types of exercise (as a gym might do), focus on the activities they do every day—especially walking—and allow them to track the impact of it and encourage more.

3 Why us? What are our sources of advantage? What trends will we ride?

- Founders' expertise in gaming methodologies.
- Ability to create simple physical devices at scale (so a pure internet-based startup could not compete).

4 User + how we will delight them. What are the two to five unique and pivotal decisions that will define of our solution?

- Make tracking exercise that is already being done easy to do.
- Build encouragement from the exercise they are already doing.
- Make it easy to set daily goals (such as 10,000 steps) and use the fact that by any given evening, they'll already be close to their goal as a mechanism to get the extra 1,000 steps or so.
- Allow them to see progress over time, earn badges, and feel good about what they are doing (as opposed to gyms and weigh-ins that are a mixture of positive and negative experiences).
- Build in social aspects—for example, allow them to have friendly competitions with friends and family.

In the Southwest example, note the four top-level bullets in section four are the "two to five unique and pivotal decisions of our solution".

The "such as…" examples in the lower-level bullets are the specific activities. Not having meals is not part of a strategy. It is an example, among many, that reinforce a commitment to limited passenger services and being low cost. Not having meals means also that they don't have to wait for a lot of food to be loaded at the gate. That's possible because they only fly short distances and it helps make the door-to-door faster as well. Southwest's four unique and pivotal decisions are coordinated.

What strategy experts often overlook

I'll also point out that all four decisions follow a natural storyline. Once they established the core concept of short routes to compete with driving, then deciding to be low cost made sense. Flying into smaller airports was a natural decision as well. And so they followed the thread to establish a full list.

The examples in Section four are important. They give the strategy real punch. But you need not have figured them all out on Day One. This is something that experts either miss or overlook explaining. As much as I'm a big fan of both Michael Porter and Kim and Mauborgne's Blue Ocean Strategy, neither one observes this in their analysis of Southwest.

The *Blue Ocean Strategy* book, for example, introduces a "strategy canvas". This is a set of five to ten customer-facing attributes that each competitor is scored on. For Southwest, the list includes lounges, meals, and hub connectivity.

Michael Porter has the "activity map" with eighteen activities in the graph. I have two issues with the activity map:

1) Showing these details that way makes them appear as if they have always existed and were prescribed in advance. (In fairness, Porter's activity maps often have major/hub and minor/spoke activities colored differently. In that case, the major ones are the "two to five unique and pivotal decisions"; the minor/spoke ones match the sub-bullet "such as…" items. Though Porter himself doesn't explain the development of a strategy as such.)
2) I see people confused about what to put in activity maps. In *Playing to Win*, an otherwise great book on P&G's strategic evolution, the P&G activity map listed are sources of advantage (e.g. "scale", "innovation", "go to-market capabilities", "customer understanding")—not decisions made. And the co-author of the strategy and book is a long-time consultant of Porter's own consulting firm, Monitor!

Why is it important to get the guiding principles and not a full list of all the specific tactics? For one, listing out the ten ways you will compete can't always be possible on Day One of a startup. You need to learn them over time. For another, not everyone in the company can remember all ten in their heads, thus violating the "keep-it-short" rule.

And finally, a company like Southwest learns over time. It wants all of its employees out there thinking about new ways to reinforce these approaches. Provide a list of ten detailed ideas to your employees and it will always stay ten. Provide four governing thoughts and your employees will give you hundreds of new specific ideas. Toyota made their Toyota Production System a strategy because they made it strategic and evolutionary while none of the other automakers did; others simply tried to copy specific parts of the system they observed.

Is Strategy Dead?

The CEO of a 500-employee company said to me recently, "strategy isn't even a full-time job here".

He was in a company that had been doing well. Why does he need strategy?

For startups, hasn't the recent rise of the Minimum Viable Product/Lean Startup approach killed the need for a strategy? Can't we figure out everything we need to know along the way, based on fast user feedback loops?

When thinking about strategy nowadays, if you're not confused, you're probably at least a bit disheartened.

I've been thinking about strategy a lot myself in recent years, first as a McKinsey consultant, and then, more recently, as a founder, strategy leader, and board director in several tech startups and growth stage companies. I wanted to share a few insights I've arrived at along the way about strategy and why it's as relevant as ever today.

There are some insights about strategy I've arrived at:

Strategy isn't dead. In fact, it's as critical today as ever

- The fact that the world is changing around us means that companies can no longer rely on annual strategic plans to provide meaningful guidance. But it also means that, without a simple articulation of whom we serve and why we create unique value for those customers, companies can become lost in the noise of a frenetic and chaotic environment around us.
- Unfortunately, collectively we have disregarded strategy in recent years. This may be because we either overestimated our ability to repeat past growth or because we have seen strategy as something far scarier than it really is. Here's a way to test this latter theory: see how quickly you can strike fear into the heart of any career executive by walking up to them and asking, "What's your strategy?"

The concept of "competitive advantage" isn't dead

- There are many great points made in the popular book whose title declared the end of competitive advantage but I disagree with its central thesis. I believe even the author disagrees with it. In her case study of Milliken, for example, she highlights their consistent distinctiveness in specialty materials production, corporate culture, and employee engagement, among other areas—all of which sound like great examples of competitive advantage to me!

- Everyone agrees the world is moving faster today than ever before. Thirty-year advantages in the 1970s may have been commonplace, while five to ten years may be more the case today. In addition, sources of competitive advantage have migrated from physical assets (e.g. mines and plants) to technical and cultural/skill-based ones. But that doesn't mean the concepts are irrelevant. Innovation today is the process of taking the set of things you do well as an organization and injecting them into new products and better ways to serve your customers.
- Find what unique technologies, skills, or resources you have that allow you to help your customers accomplish things 2-, 3-, 5-, or 10-times faster, cheaper, or better than they otherwise could: that's why they're buying from you and that's where your advantage lies. If you don't have a competitive advantage, why is anyone buying your product?

The Lean Startup approach has not made strategy irrelevant. In fact, one without the other is dangerous, and the two combined are exceptionally powerful

- The Lean Startup approach is a set of tools and concepts to create highly-mobile teams that iterate the product development cycle. But too many startups are using quick iterations and Minimum Viable Products as an excuse to avoid upfront strategic thinking.
- If you iterate purely on an MPV without the guidance of a strategy, who knows if you'll end up solving a need large enough to be meaningful to buyers?

Google's success has not proven that strategy is irrelevant

- Google is distinctive at hiring creative, smart engineers, investing large amounts of money in long-term products, and creating technical, web-based solutions in easy-to-use products. The ability to do those things is a large part of their competitive advantage.
- Google's two most public failures, Wave (a real-time email and messaging platform) and Glass (wearable glasses) were anchored in those areas of competitive advantage.
- They were both built on a technical insight but solved no articulated business need. They probably iterated the product development with a Lean Startup approach and got great user feedback. But then what problem did they solve? For whom? Why would anyone pay (or accept advertisements) for them? Strategy forces these questions into the forefront.

Analytics is the root of most effective strategies today

- Years ago, strategy was anchored primarily in frameworks (e.g. the Five Forces) and executive muscle memory. Those days are gone. Strategy today needs to be heavily anchored in data. Data is the best guide we have to strategic decisions and investments—especially data that we can uniquely see.

- In addition, building an analytics flywheel into your product to inform new waves of innovation and customer value over time is a powerful component of a strategy.

The three primary colors of building a business are Strategy + Analytics + Agility

- Strategy is a clear vision of whom you are serving, the problem you are solving for them, an understanding of why they need your help solving it, and an outline of how you'll solve it.
- Analytics (or a similar technological insight) is the unique tool that you are able to use to solve the problem that others either don't have access to or haven't considered applying to this problem.
- Agility is your unique ability to quickly deploy the technology to solve the problem for the customer, get feedback, and continuously improve.

Hiring and investing in "strategic stem cells" is a primary way that companies can become more mobile, innovate faster, and be able to re-allocate resources as needed

- When startups and successful companies are hiring today, they look for people who are comfortable with ambiguity, can learn new skills, and who get excited about the prospect of playing multiple roles in their company. They look to make deep investments in core assets that can evolve into different products as an uncertain future plays out (e.g. flexible factories). They double down on building fundamental capabilities such as customer care, designing unique user experiences, and training their employees.
- These are all examples of what I call "strategic stem cells": the flexible collection of skills/assets/capabilities that can be moved into different products as corporate priorities shift in a fast-evolving environment.
- Like a blank tile in Scrabble, strategic stem cells can play the role of any vowel. What's the word we'll need? Patting? Putting? Potting? Our future options are open.

Companies need to be decentralized and agile to innovate ... and a strong, simple strategy will let you do it

- My personal affinity is to the startup model where everything is both centralized and decentralized at the same time: the firm is small enough so everyone can see and weigh in on most things quickly, while any employee is typically afforded the freedom to propose and run with major changes. But even in startups, I've seen the pendulum swing, as it should. There's a period of open innovation where solutions are cobbled together (in a decentralized way), then, once the proof points are established, there's a period of purposeful rebuilding to handle scale, maintain consistency, and improve responsiveness (as part of a centralized build).

- When I've had the chance to be part of larger companies, I've seen how hard it is to let any process run in a decentralized way. Any company looking to be more innovative has to reduce the centralization of control. There are many ways to do it. The most important criteria is that they have a strong, simple strategy. Then decentralized, agile teams can operate with the freedom they need within the confines of a consistent corporate direction.

The existence of "Black Swans" underscores the need for short, simple, and thoughtful strategies

- Nassim Nicholas Taleb's popular books on "Black Swans", the rare and extreme events whose odds of occurring are unknowable, provide no justification for avoiding having a strategy. Indeed, a strategy is most valuable in those situations. A strategy should provide enough clarity during the chaos of shocks to your market while still being open-ended enough to allow all employees to adjust their own decisions and actions as needed as the exact circumstances and opportunities evolve.

Further resources and acknowledgements

Chapter 1

- Corporate portfolio strategy
    - Viguerie, Patrick et al., 2008, *The Granularity of Growth,* McKinsey & Company.
        - One note: the authors claim the goal should be to re-allocate resources to any pockets of growth, not just profitable pockets. They assert that profitability inevitably follows volume. That is a controversial statement. Focusing on pockets of profitable growth (or at least pockets where there is a clear path to profitability) will help you avoid the pitfalls that airlines, for example, have fallen into, where there's a long history of investing in high-volume routes that nonetheless consistently degrade the overall profits of the company.
    - Bradley, Chris, et al., 2018, *Strategy Beyond the Hockey Stick*, McKinsey & Company.
    - Zenger, Todd, 2016, *Beyond Competitive Advantage: How to Solve the Puzzle of Sustaining Growth While Creating Value*, Harvard Business Review Press.
        - The Disney case study mentioned above is in chapter one.
- General strategy
    - Bradley, Chris, et al., 2013, *Mastering the Building Blocks of Strategy,* McKinsey Quarterly 2013 Issue #4. Available at: http://www.mckinsey.com/business-functions/strategy-and-corporate-finance/our-insights/mastering-the-building-blocks-of-strategy
    - Porter, Michael, 1985, *Competitive Advantage*, Free Press
    - Porter, Michael, 1996 and re-published in 2011, *"What is Strategy?" from HBR's "On Strategy"*
    - Porter, Michael, 1998, *Competitive Strategy,* Free Press
    - Magretta, Joan, 2011, *Understanding Michael Porter*, Harvard Business Review Press

Chapter 2

- Sharp, Isadore, 2012, *Four Seasons: The Story of a Business Philosophy.*
- General strategy
    - Bradley, Chris, et al., 2013, *Mastering the Building Blocks of Strategy,* McKinsey Quarterly 2013 Issue #4. Available at: http://www.mckinsey.com/business-functions/strategy-and-corporate-finance/our-insights/mastering-the-building-blocks-of-strategy
    - Porter, Michael, 1985, *Competitive Advantage*, Free Press
    - Porter, Michael, 1996 and re-published in 2011, *"What is Strategy?" from HBR's "On Strategy"*

- Porter, Michael, 1998, *Competitive Strategy,* Free Press
- Magretta, Joan, 2011, *Understanding Michael Porter*, Harvard Business Review Press
- Special thanks to Jason Majane for his expertise.

Chapter 3

- Mauborgne, Renée and Kim, W. Chan, 2004, *Blue Ocean Strategy*

Chapter 4

- https://www.mckinsey.com/business-functions/strategy-and-corporate-finance/our-insights/the-strategic-yardstick-you-cant-afford-to-ignore
- https://www.mckinsey.com/industries/high-tech/our-insights/how-tech-giants-deliver-outsized-returns-and-what-it-means-for-the-rest-of-us

Chapter 5

- Lafley, A.G. and Martin, Roger L., 2013, *Playing to Win: How Strategy Really Works*, Harvard Business Review Press. (The Olay example comes from chapter one; the buyer versus user example from chapter six).

Chapter 6

- Mauborgne, Renée and Kim, W. Chan, 2004, *Blue Ocean Strategy*
- Lafley, A.G. and Martin, Roger L., 2013, *Playing to Win: How Strategy Really Works*, Harvard Business Review Press. (The Olay example comes from chapter one; the buyer versus user example from chapter six).

Chapter 7

- McGrath, Rita Gunther, 2013, *The End of Competitive Advantage: How to Keep Your Strategy Moving as Fast as Your Business*, Harvard Business Review Press.
    - The Milliken case study mentioned above is in chapter two.
- Taleb, Nassim Nicholas, 2007, *The Black Swan: The Impact of the Highly Improbable*, Random House.

Made in United States
Orlando, FL
21 April 2023

32325799R00027